# CANCUN
# TRAVEL GUIDE 2023

*A Tourist's Guide to a Memorable Carribean Getaway*

**Paul Dillard**

1

# Dedication

To our valued readers,

We dedicate this travel guide to you, our dear travelers, who have made it possible for us to share our passion for exploration and adventure. We hope that this guide serves as a trusted companion on your journey to Cancun, providing you with valuable insights and insider tips to make your trip unforgettable.

We also extend our gratitude to the hardworking individuals who have contributed to making Cancun the beautiful destination that it is today. From the locals who warmly welcome visitors to the staff at the hotels and attractions who work tirelessly to provide exceptional experiences, we appreciate your dedication and commitment to the tourism industry.

Thank you for choosing to embark on this journey with us. We wish you a safe and fulfilling adventure in Cancun.

Paul Dillard, 2023. .

# Table of Contents

# I. About Cancun

## Brief history of Cancun

A seaside city in Mexico's southeast is called Cancun. The Mayan name for the city was Ekab, which translates to "black earth" in English. The region was long populated by the Mayans, who used it as a major jade and other precious stone trade hub.

Spanish conquistadors landed in the region in the 16th century and built a small harbor. But until the 20th century, when the Mexican government started to realize Cancun's potential as a tourist destination, the region was mostly disregarded.

The Mexican government came up with a strategy in 1967 to turn Cancun into a premier tourism destination. The government made significant investments in infrastructure, constructing a world-class airport, roadways, and lodging facilities. The Playa Blanca, the first hotel, debuted in 1974.

Cancun's growth required a significant effort since the region was mostly unpopulated and lacked the requisite infrastructure. A thorough development plan was developed by the government in collaboration with private businesses and called for the building of opulent hotels and resorts as well as retail malls and other facilities.

The strategy worked, and Cancun swiftly rose to prominence as one of Mexico's top tourist attractions. Cancun now has a robust tourism business that draws millions of tourists from all over the globe each year.

Despite its popularity, Cancun has had several difficulties throughout time. The city suffered severe damage from Hurricane Wilma in 2005, which also led to the destruction of numerous hotels and other structures. The city has subsequently rebounded, however, and is a popular tourist attraction once again.

Cancun has recently had difficulties with safety and security due to allegations of drug-related crime and violence. Although the government has taken action to solve these problems, tourists looking for sun, sand, and leisure continue to flock to the city.

Cancun is renowned for its rich cultural legacy in addition to its stunning beaches. Numerous historic Mayan ruins, including the well-known Chichen Itza and Tulum, can be found in the city. These ruins, which are well-liked tourist destinations, provide a look into the earlier Mayan civilisation.

Cancun is renowned for having a thriving entertainment and nightlife scene. There are many different restaurants, pubs, and nightclubs in the city, catering to various interests and price ranges. There are many possibilities in Cancun, whether you're searching for a romantic candlelit supper for two or a crazy night out with friends.

The Day of the Dead, a Mexican celebration observed in early November, is one of the most significant occasions in Cancun's cultural calendar. Locals and tourists alike gather at this time to remember their departed loved ones. There are parades, live music performances, various activities, and beautiful altars all across the city.

The tourist industry is a major contributor to Cancun's economy, and the city has developed and grown throughout time. To keep the city a popular tourism destination, the government has made investments in facilities and infrastructure.

Cancun continues to be a beautiful and energetic city with a rich history and culture despite the difficulties it has encountered. Cancun has something for everyone, whether you're seeking for a trip by the beach, an adventure in the jungle, or a peek into Mexico's distant history.

## What makes Cancun worth visiting in 2023?

There are many good reasons to go to Mexico's Cancun in 2023. There is something for everyone in this coastal city, from its stunning beaches and lively culture to its top-notch food and diverse nightlife. Just a few reasons to think about making Cancun your next holiday spot are listed below:

## Stunning beaches

Cancun is well known for having some of the nicest beaches in the world. The beaches in Cancun are the ideal spot to unwind and enjoy the sun since they have beautiful, blue seas and smooth, white sand. Cancun has everything you're searching for, from a quiet place to read a book to a wild beach party.

At the southernmost point of the Hotel Zone, Playa Delfines is one of Cancun's busiest beaches. The area is well-known for its breathtaking vistas and turquoise seas, which make it the ideal location for swimming, tanning, and even surfing. The renowned

"Cancun" sign is also located on the beach, where tourists may snap pictures to remember their vacation.

Playa Norte, another well-liked beach, is situated on the northernmost point of Isla Mujeres, a tiny island off the coast of Cancun. Families with small children will love this beach's tranquil seas and beautiful, white sand because of this. The beach is a perfect spot to unwind and have a drink or meal while admiring the breathtaking views since it is also home to a number of pubs and restaurants.

There are several secret beaches in Cancun to explore for those seeking a more private setting. Playa Maroma, which can be found approximately 30 minutes south of Cancun, is one of the most stunning. This beach is ideal for a romantic break since it gives a more private experience and has beautiful white sand and lovely waves.

The beaches in Cancun offer a variety of additional activities besides swimming and tanning. Numerous beaches provide water activities including jet skiing, parasailing, snorkeling, and scuba diving. In addition, one of the several marinas in the region offers fishing trips and sunset cruises.

Last but not least, Cancun's beaches provide breathtaking views of the Caribbean Sea and the surrounding area. The beaches in Cancun provide a stunning background for your holiday, whether you're taking in the dawn or the sunset. So the Cancun beaches are a must-go location whether you're seeking solace, excitement, or simply some breathtaking views.

## Rich culture

Cancun has a rich cultural heritage, with ancient Mayan ruins, traditional Mexican cuisine, and vibrant festivals and celebrations. Visit the ruins of Chichen Itza or Tulum to learn about the ancient Mayan civilization, or sample the delicious flavors of traditional Mexican cuisine in one of the city's many restaurants.

One of the most iconic symbols of Cancun's culture is the ancient Mayan ruins that are scattered throughout the region. Some of the most popular ruins include Chichen Itza and Tulum, which offer a glimpse into the fascinating history and architecture of the Mayan civilization. Visitors can explore the temples, pyramids, and other structures that were built centuries ago, and learn about the culture and traditions of this ancient civilization.

Another way to experience Cancun's rich culture is through its cuisine. Mexican cuisine is world-renowned, and Cancun is no exception. The city is home to many traditional restaurants that offer a variety of dishes, from tacos and burritos to ceviche and guacamole. Visitors can also sample local delicacies such as cochinita pibil, a slow-roasted pork dish, and churros, a sweet pastry that is popular in Mexico.

In addition to its ancient ruins and traditional cuisine, Cancun is also home to many festivals and celebrations that showcase the region's culture. One of the most popular is the Day of the Dead, which is celebrated throughout Mexico on November 1st and 2nd. During this time, locals create elaborate altars and offerings to honor their deceased loved ones, and visitors can participate in parades and other cultural events.

Other festivals and celebrations in Cancun include the Carnival of Cancun, which takes place in February or March and features parades, live music, and colorful costumes, and the Independence Day celebration on September 16th, which is marked by fireworks, parades, and traditional Mexican food and drinks.

Cancun's rich culture offers visitors a unique and diverse experience that is deeply rooted in its ancient Mayan heritage and its history as a Spanish colony. Whether you're exploring ancient ruins, sampling traditional Mexican cuisine, or participating in local festivals and celebrations, there are countless ways to experience Cancun's vibrant culture.

## Fun activities

Cancun has a lot to offer if adventure is what you're after. There are many exhilarating things to attempt in Cancun, from swimming with dolphins to zip-lining through the jungle. A number of amusement parks, including Xcaret and Xel-Ha, are also located in the city and provide a range of activities for visitors of all ages.

Cancun is known for its water sports, and the area's warm, clear seas are ideal for activities like snorkeling, scuba diving, and jet skiing. Scuba divers may explore the second-largest barrier reef system in the world, the famed Mesoamerican Barrier Reef, which is home to a wide variety of marine life, including colorful fish, sea turtles, and even sharks.

Parasailing and windsurfing are well-liked sports in Cancun for anyone who would rather remain on dry land. While windsurfing enables you to ride the waves and get an adrenaline rush, parasailing allows you to fly above the water and take in breath-taking vistas of the coastline.

Cancun is a fantastic location for outdoor activities as well. Numerous natural parks and reserves may be found in the Yucatan Peninsula, giving tourists the chance to experience the area's diverse biodiversity. In addition to giving tourists the ability to see animals, swim in subterranean rivers, and learn about traditional Mexican culture via music and dance performances, Xcaret Park is a well-liked destination that mixes nature and culture.

The Selvatica Adventure Park, which provides a variety of activities including ziplining, ATV trips, and swimming in cenotes, is another well-liked destination. Visitors may enjoy the rush of riding an ATV across the tough terrain or zipping through the forest on a zipline.

A must-do activity for anybody interested in learning more about the area's rich history is a visit to the ancient Mayan ruins. Within a few hours of Cancun, travelers may explore the intriguing history and culture of the Mayan civilisation at the ruins of Chichen Itza, Tulum, and Coba.

Numerous adventurous activities are available in Cancun for all kinds of tourists. There are many thrilling adventures to be gained in this lovely location, including water sports, outdoor pursuits, and touring historic ruins.

## Vibrant Nightlife

Cancun is renowned for having a thriving nightlife with a wide variety of bars, clubs, and restaurants. You can find everything in Cancun, whether you're searching for a quiet drink with pals or a crazy night out. It is simple to find a party no matter where you are staying since many of the city's pubs and clubs are situated in the Hotel Zone.

The Hotel Zone is a stretch of beachfront hotels and resorts in Cancun that is home to several restaurants and nightclubs. It is one of the most well-known destinations for nightlife. The City, one of the biggest clubs in Latin America, is renowned for its cutting-edge sound system and famous patrons, while The Coco Bongo is a famed nightclub with live performances and exciting dance acts.

Cancun also has a selection of lounges and bars for individuals who prefer a more laid-back setting. La Vaquita and Mandala are bustling bars with a joyful and dynamic environment, while the rooftop bars of the Grand Fiesta Americana and the Thompson Hotel are well-liked places to drink cocktails and watch the sunset.

Beyond merely drinking and dancing, Cancun also provides a wide range of entertainment opportunities. A popular attraction that blends acrobatics, music, and theater is called Joya by Cirque du Soleil. It offers a unique and amazing experience. Additionally, live music performances are offered at places including The City, Mandala, and Daddy O.

Cancun's downtown area is also home to a large number of pubs and nightclubs that provide a more local and genuine experience in addition to the Hotel Zone. Local brews and tequilas are often consumed in the El Centro district, where pubs like Las de Guanatos and El Rincón del Vino provide a relaxed ambiance.

One of Cancun's biggest draws is its vibrant nightlife, which provides guests with a range of ways to enjoy food, drink, and entertainment. Everyone may find something to enjoy in this dynamic location, which offers everything from energized dance clubs to relaxed lounges and neighborhood pubs.

**Natural beauty**
Cancun is home to a number of natural parks and reserves, including the Isla Contoy National Park and the Sian Ka'an Biosphere Reserve, in addition to its lovely beaches. Visitors may enjoy the natural beauty of the area in these

places, which are home to a diverse diversity of flora and animals.

The beaches of Cancun, which are among the most stunning in the world, are among the city's most well-known natural features. A picture-perfect scene for swimming, sunbathing, and water sports is created by the Caribbean Sea's pristine white beach and azure seas. Playa Delfines, Playa Tortugas, and Playa Norte are among of Cancun's busiest beaches; each has a distinct personality and allure.

Cancun has a lot of natural parks and reserves that provide tourists the ability to experience the area's many ecosystems in addition to its beaches. A well-liked attraction that has subterranean rivers, unusual creatures, and authentic Mexican shows is called Xcaret Park. A UNESCO World Heritage site that preserves a wide variety of flora and wildlife is the Sian Ka'an Biosphere Reserve, while Xel-Há Park is a natural aquarium that allows snorkeling and swimming with marine life.

The Yucatan Peninsula provides a range of outdoor excursions for people who wish to enjoy the area's untamed splendor. The Mayan ruins of Chichen Itza, Tulum, and Coba provide a look into the area's rich history and culture against a background of lush tropical woods and untamed limestone formations. Cenotes, or natural sinkholes, are another distinctive natural feature with waters that are ideal for diving, swimming, and snorkeling.

The region's waterways are also home to a variety of marine life, thus Cancun's natural beauty is not confined to its land-based attractions. The Mesoamerican Barrier Reef, the second-largest barrier reef system in the world, offers a spectacular underwater world of colorful fish, coral reefs, and sea turtles. Snorkeling and scuba diving are popular activities in Cancun.

Visitors are drawn in large numbers by Cancun's natural beauty, which includes a variety of breathtaking vistas that highlight the area's distinctive geology, vegetation, and wildlife. There are many natural delights to discover in this stunning location, from pristine beaches and crystal-clear lakes to lush tropical jungles and craggy mountain ranges.

## Accessibility

Many significant American and Canadian cities have direct flights to and from Cancun International Airport, making it simple to get to

Cancun from these locations. A few hours' travel separates the city from other well-known Mexican tourist spots like Tulum and Playa del Carmen.

With direct flights to and from a large number of important places in North America, South America, Europe, and Asia, Cancun International Airport is one of the busiest airports in Mexico for travelers coming by air. The Hotel Zone and downtown Cancun are both close to the airport, making it simple for guests to go to their lodgings and begin their holiday right away.

Visitors have a selection of transportation alternatives once they arrive in Cancun. The city is filled with taxis and ride-sharing companies like Uber and Cabify, which provide a simple and inexpensive way to get about. A lot of the lodging establishments in the Hotel Zone also provide shuttle services to well-known tourist sites and commercial districts.

Cancun's public transportation is also readily available and simple to use. With regular service and reasonable charges, the city's well-developed bus system travels through the Hotel Zone and downtown Cancun. The CancunRide bus service, which provides direct connections to well-liked sites and locations all around the area, is another option for tourists.

There are also several transportation choices accessible for people who desire to go outside of Cancun. Major rental agencies are extensively distributed around the city, including the airport. Visitors may also benefit from guided tours and excursions, which provide access to well-liked locations like the Mayan ruins and natural parks as well as knowledgeable guides.

The accessibility of Cancun is a huge benefit for tourists, with a variety of transportation choices that make it simple to travel about and discover all the area has to offer. Visitors can easily traverse the city and enjoy all of its many sights and activities whether they arrive by flight, use cabs and ride-sharing services, or rely on the city's public transit system.

**Luxurious lodging**

Some of the most opulent hotels and resorts in the world, including those with private beaches, spas, and fine dining establishments, can be found in Cancun. Cancun offers a wide range of possibilities, whether you're seeking for a romantic break or a family holiday.

The Hotel Zone, where a wide range of resorts and hotels line the lovely beaches and provide breathtaking views of the Caribbean Sea, is the primary location for upscale lodging in Cancun. There are alternatives for every taste and budget among these places, which vary from large all-inclusive resorts to boutique hotels and opulent villas.

Numerous resorts in Cancun provide top-notch facilities and services, including a variety of dining options, bars, swimming pools, spas, fitness centers, and recreational activities. These establishments are also renowned for their top-notch customer care, with helpful staff members that go above and beyond to provide each visitor a memorable and pleasurable stay.

The city and surrounding neighborhoods of Cancun, as well as other regions outside the Hotel Zone, provide upscale lodging options. These venues give guests a variety of alternatives for their stay in Cancun, ranging from modest boutique hotels to opulent villas and private houses.

Many of these establishments offer their visitors exceptional experiences and services in addition to the luxurious lodgings itself. Private beach access, individualized butler service, fine dining occasions, and exclusive trips and activities are a few examples.

A wide variety of opulent lodging alternatives are available in Cancun, catering to every taste and price range. Visitors may luxuriate in the utmost in luxury and convenience while taking in the stunning natural surroundings and rich culture of this magnificent area, in world-class resorts or private villas.

In summary, Cancun is a beautiful and energetic city that offers something for everyone. There is no lack of things to do and see in Cancun, from its breathtaking beaches and vibrant culture to its exhilarating adventure offerings and first-rate nightlife. Cancun is the ideal location for your 2023 holiday, whether you're seeking for excitement or leisure.

# II. Getting to Cancun in 2023

Detailed analysis, evaluation and information about the various ways of getting to Cancun in 2023 8s provided in this Chapter.

## 1. By air

With direct flights from various places across the globe to Cancun's international airport, flying is often the quickest and most convenient option for guests.

Numerous airlines provide direct flights to Cancun International Airport (CUN) from significant locations in North America, South America, Europe, and Asia, making it simple and hassle-free to travel to Cancun by air. There are several airlines that provide direct flights to Cancun, whether you're travelling from New

York or Los Angeles, Toronto or Vancouver, London or Paris, or even Tokyo or Beijing.

American Airlines, Delta Air Lines, United Airlines, Air Canada, WestJet, British Airways, Lufthansa, Air France, KLM, and Japan Airlines are just a few of the well-known carriers that provide direct flights to Cancun. These airlines provide solutions to fit every budget and desire with a variety of pricing and service levels, including economy, business, and first class.

Visitors can easily go to their hotels and begin their holiday since the airport is conveniently close to the Hotel Zone and downtown Cancun. The airport provides a variety of services and conveniences, such as currency exchange, duty-free shopping, dining options, and vehicle rental options.

Customs and immigration must be cleared by travelers arriving at Cancun International Airport, which might take some time during busy travel times. Visitors may pick up their bags after clearing customs and then go to the transportation hub to take a shuttle, cab, or ride-sharing service to their lodging.

It's crucial to remember that travelers entering Mexico must have a valid passport and, depending on their place of origin, may also need to get a tourist visa or travel permit. Additionally, travelers should research any entrance requirements and travel warnings for their trip and get travel insurance to be covered in case of emergencies or unforeseen circumstances.

Numerous airlines provide direct flights to Cancun International Airport from significant locations all over the globe, making it simple and easy to get to Cancun by air. Visitors may choose from a variety of airlines, prices, and service levels, and take advantage of a hassle-free journey that whisks them away to one of the most breathtaking and exciting holiday spots on the planet.

## 2. Through land

Although flying is a well-liked method of travel, there are various choices for those who would rather drive or take a bus to get to Cancun.

Those who reside in nearby cities or regions, as well as those who prefer the convenience of having their own vehicle for exploring the area, have the option of driving to Cancun. The Yucatan Peninsula and other adjacent locations may be readily reached by automobile from the city because to its well-maintained highways and roads, which provide for a pleasant and picturesque journey. Visitors should be aware that certain roadways may have tolls and should get acquainted with the local driving laws and rules.

Taking a bus is an additional means of travel to get to Cancun from land. There are numerous significant bus companies in Mexico that provide service to Cancun from cities all over the nation, with prices ranging from inexpensive to more luxurious and comfortable. ADO, OCC, and Mayab are a few of the main bus companies that provide service to Cancun.

The Cancun bus station is situated in the city's center and provides quick access to the Hotel Zone and other parts of the city.

Depending on where they are starting from, travelers can also travel to Cancun by train or ferry. Merida is the city with the closest railway station to Cancun, and driving there takes around 4 hours. Additionally, there are ferry services that link Cancun to nearby islands and places like Cozumel and Isla Mujeres.

Regardless of the route travelers take to get to Cancun by land, it's crucial to prepare and take the necessary safety precautions. These include checking traffic conditions and safety advisories, carrying the proper identification and documentation, and buying travel insurance to cover unforeseen circumstances.

Although flying is a popular way to get to Cancun, there are also a number of options for people who would rather drive or take a bus. Visitors can take a scenic drive or a relaxing bus ride to get to this stunning and energetic vacation spot, which is close to the city's beautiful beaches, a thriving cultural scene, and a wealth of activities and attractions.

## 3. By sea

For tourists who enjoy cruising or boating, traveling to Cancun by sea is a novel and exciting option. There are still a few options available for those who want to travel by sea, even though it's not a common way to get to the city.

Taking a cruise ship with a stop in Cancun included is one way to travel by sea to the destination. Cancun is a stop on many major cruise lines' itineraries, and the city's port provides quick access to the Hotel Zone and other parts of the city. Before continuing on their cruise itinerary, visitors can spend the day enjoying the city's beaches, landmarks, and recreational opportunities.

Renting a private yacht or boat is another way to travel to Cancun by sea. For those who prefer to travel at their own pace and on their own schedule, this option is ideal. There are various yacht and boat rental businesses in Cancun that provide a variety of alternatives, from tiny boats to luxury yachts, with or without a crew.

Visitors who are going from adjacent places, such as the Caribbean or the Gulf of Mexico, may also be able to reach Cancun by their own boat or yacht. The city's marinas provide abundant mooring space and services for boaters, with convenient access to the Hotel Zone and other regions of the city.

Regardless of how travelers choose to reach Cancun by water, it's crucial to prepare ahead and take required measures, such as monitoring weather and sea conditions, carrying suitable papers and identification, and familiarizing oneself with the local boating rules and regulations.

In conclusion, although not a frequent means to approach the city, accessing Cancun by water may be a unique and interesting choice for those who prefer cruise or boating. Visitors may board a cruise ship, hire a private yacht or boat, or come by their own boat or yacht from surrounding areas, experiencing the city's magnificent beaches, rich culture, and wealth of activities and sights from a unique and unforgettable viewpoint.

# III. Where to Stay in Cancun in 2023

Whether you are on a tight budget or have a lot to spend, let us help you find the best accommodation for a hassle - free memorable journey.

## 1. Types of accommodation available in Cancun

Cancun is a well-known holiday spot with a wide variety of lodging alternatives to fit all interests and budgets. There are plenty of places to stay in Cancun, from opulent resorts to inexpensive hostels. Some of the most well-liked lodging options in the city are listed below:

## Luxurious Resorts

Cancun is well renowned for its opulent resorts, many of which are situated in the Hotel Zone. These resorts provide a wide range of facilities and services, including exclusive beaches, swimming areas, spas, dining options, and bars. The Ritz-Carlton, Live Aqua Beach Resort Cancun, and Secrets The Vine Cancun are a few of the city's most well-known luxury properties.

## All- inclusive Resorts

Many of the resorts in Cancun are all-inclusive, which means that visitors pay a single price that includes their lodging, food, beverages, and the majority of activities. This is a fantastic choice for those who wish to take a trip without any hassles or extra costs. The Moon Palace Cancun, Hard Rock Hotel Cancun, and Grand Fiesta Americana Coral Beach Cancun are a few of the most well-known all-inclusive hotels in Cancun.

## Boutique Hotels

There are a number of boutique hotels in Cancun for tourists that desire a more individualized and private experience. These hotels often have a smaller footprint, distinctive interior design, and individualized service. In Cancun, some of the most well-liked boutique hotels include Hotel Le Blanc Spa Resort, Nizuc Resort & Spa, and Casa Turquesa.

## Vacation Rentals

Vacation rentals are a fantastic choice for those who wish to experience staying in a home away from home. In Cancun, there are several places to rent a holiday home, including flats, condominiums, and villas. These lodgings often include complete kitchens, enabling visitors to prepare their own meals and spend less money eating out. Airbnb, VRBO, and HomeAway are a few of the most well-known websites for booking vacation rentals in Cancun.

**Hostels**

Cancun is home to various hostels that provide inexpensive lodging for those on a tight budget. These hostels often include private rooms for individuals who want more privacy in addition to dormitory-style rooms with common toilets. Hostel Natura, Mayan Monkey Hostel, and Selina Cancun Downtown are a few of the most well-liked hostels in Cancun.

## Bed and Breakfasts

There are various bed and breakfasts in Cancun for tourists looking for a more cozy and pleasant setting. These establishments often provide cozy lodging with complimentary breakfast. Villa Italia Bed & Breakfast, Casa Mexicana Cancun, and Casa Ixchel Cancun are a few of the most well-known bed and breakfasts in Cancun.

## Timeshares

If you want to visit Cancun regularly, timeshares are a fantastic choice. Timeshares provide visitors the chance to purchase a section of a hotel or condo and use it for a certain amount of time each year. Long-term, this might be a terrific method to save costs on lodging. The Marriott Vacation Club and the Westin Lagunamar Ocean Resort are two of the most well-liked timeshare choices in Cancun.

In conclusion, Cancun provides a variety of lodging choices to meet all tastes and price ranges. There are plenty of places to stay in this lovely holiday spot, from opulent resorts to inexpensive hostels. Cancun offers both leisurely getaways and action-packed vacations, so there is something for everyone.

## 2. Best locations to stay in Cancin in 2023

There are several neighborhoods to pick from in Cancun, a well-liked holiday spot, when it comes to locating the ideal location to stay. It's crucial to choose the region that most closely matches your requirements and interests since each neighborhood has its own own characteristics and advantages. Some of the top places to stay in Cancun are listed below:

## The Hotel Zone

Tourists choose to stay in Cancun's Hotel Zone more than any other region. It is a long, slender stretch of land that is surrounded on one side by the Caribbean Sea and on the other by a lagoon. The majority of the big resorts, eateries, and entertainment venues are located in this neighborhood. Additionally, some of Cancun's most stunning beaches are located there. For individuals who don't mind crowds and want to be near to the action, this location is fantastic.

## Downtown Cancun

For anyone looking to immerse themselves in the local lifestyle and see Mexico as it really is, Downtown Cancun is a fantastic destination. It is around 15 minutes away from the Hotel Zone and has a large number of regional stores, marketplaces, and dining establishments. Many of the city's historic sites and institutions, such the Iglesia de Cristo Rey and the Cancun Museum of Anthropology, are located in downtown Cancun. This region is excellent for anyone who wish to explore the city and learn about the local way of life.

## Puerto Cancun

Just to the north of the Hotel Zone, Puerto Cancun is a more recent construction. A golf course, a marina, a retail mall, and opulent residences and villas are all part of this private enclave. For individuals who like to remain in a more premium residential neighborhood while yet being near to the excitement, this region is fantastic.

## Isla Mujeres

Isla Mujeres is a little island that lies close to Cancun's shore. Beautiful beaches and a laid-back ambiance are among its top attractions. For those who prefer to avoid the crowds and have a more tranquil, relaxed holiday, this region is fantastic. From Cancun, a boat travels to Isla Mujeres, where there are a variety of accommodations to select from.

## Playa Mujeres

To the north of the Hotel Zone is a more recent construction project called Playa Mujeres. In addition to a golf course and marina, it is home to numerous opulent resorts and villas. For those who wish to stay in a more upmarket, peaceful neighborhood that is yet near to the excitement, this place is fantastic.

## Tulum

About two hours south of Cancun lies the fashionable beach town of Tulum. It is renowned for its eco-friendly resorts, bohemian atmosphere, and gorgeous beaches. For those seeking a more relaxed, alternative holiday, this region is fantastic. Numerous yoga studios, organic dining establishments, and eco-friendly hotels and resorts can be found in Tulum.

**Riviera Maya**

From Cancun to Tulum, there is a coastline known as the Riviera Maya. Numerous five-star hotels, eco-friendly cabins, and little coastal villages may be found there. For those who wish to explore the area's natural splendor and have a more laid-back, off-the-beaten-path vacation, this place is fantastic.

There are several neighborhoods in Cancun to select from while looking for the ideal spot to stay. There is a location that will suit your requirements and interests, whether you want to be among the excitement in the Hotel Zone or take in the local culture in Downtown

Cancun. Cancun offers a variety of lodging options, from opulent resorts to green lodges.

## 3. Popular Resorts and Hotels

Cancun is renowned for its opulent resorts and hotels that provide breathtaking vistas, first-rate facilities, and top-notch service. Some of the most well-known resorts and hotels in Cancun are listed below:

### The Ritz-Carlton, Cancun

Situated in the Hotel Zone, this opulent beachfront property is known for its impeccable service. It has a private beach, multiple dining options, a spa, a fitness center, and 363 guest rooms and suites. Additionally, the resort provides a range of experiences and activities, such as culinary workshops, tequila tastings, and dolphin sightings.

## Secrets The Vine Cancun

Secrets An all-inclusive resort called The Vine Cancun is situated in the Hotel Zone. It has 497 guest rooms and suites, a spa, a fitness center, multiple dining options, and swimming pools. The resort is renowned for its first-rate service and opulent facilities.

## Nizuc Resort & Spa

The opulent beachside resort of Nizuc Resort & Spa is situated in Punta Nizuc, a short distance from the Hotel Zone. It has 274 guest rooms and suites, a spa, a fitness center, multiple dining options, and swimming pools. In addition, the resort includes a private beach and provides a range of adventures, such paddleboarding and snorkeling.

## Grand Fiesta Americana Coral Beach Cancun

Located in the Hotel Zone, Grand Fiesta Americana Coral Beach Cancun is an opulent beachfront resort. It has 602 guest rooms and suites, a spa, a fitness center, multiple dining options, and swimming pools. The resort is renowned for both its outstanding customer service and its breathtaking views of the Caribbean Sea.

## JW Marriott Cancun property & Spa

Located in the Hotel Zone, JW Marriott Cancun Resort & Spa is an opulent beachfront property. It has 447 guest rooms and suites, a spa, a fitness center, multiple dining options, and swimming pools. The resort is renowned for both its outstanding customer service and its breathtaking views of the Caribbean Sea.

## Hard Rock Hotel Cancun

Situated in the Hotel Zone, Hard Rock Hotel Cancun is an all-inclusive resort. It has 601 guest rooms and suites, a spa, a fitness center, multiple dining options, and swimming pools. The resort is renowned for its live entertainment and rock & roll-themed decorations.

## Hyatt Zilara Cancun

Situated in the Hotel Zone, Hyatt Zilara Cancun is an all-inclusive resort. It has a spa, a fitness facility, multiple swimming pools, various restaurants, and 307 adult-only guest rooms and suites. The resort is renowned for its first-rate service and opulent facilities.

## Live Aqua Beach Resort Cancun

This is an all-inclusive resort that is situated in the Hotel Zone. It has 371 guest rooms and suites, as well as a spa, a fitness center, and a number of swimming pools. It also has a number of restaurants and bars. The resort is renowned for its chic furnishings and opulent services.

## The Westin Lagunamar Ocean property Villas & Spa

This beachfront property is situated in the Hotel Zone. It has 592 guest rooms and villas, as well as a number of dining establishments, bars, a spa, a fitness center, and swimming pools. The resort has a kids club and a mini-golf course among other family-friendly facilities and pursuits.

## Le Blanc Spa Resort Cancun

Situated in the Hotel Zone, Le Blanc Spa Resort Cancun is an all-inclusive resort. It has 260 guest rooms and suites, a spa, a fitness center, many bars and restaurants, as well as a number of swimming pools. The resort is renowned for its first-rate service and opulent facilities.

# IV. Where to go and what to do in Cancun in 2023

## 1. Beaches and water activities

Cancun is well known for its gorgeous beaches and beautiful seas, which let tourists partake in a variety of water sports. Here are some of Cancun's most well-liked waters activities and beaches:

**Playa Delfines** is a well-known public beach with white sand and crystal-clear seas that is situated in the Hotel Zone. It is one of Cancun's biggest beaches and a well-liked location for swimming, surfing, and tanning.

**Playa Norte**: Just a short boat journey from Cancun, Playa Norte is a beautiful beach on the island of Isla Mujeres. The beach is a well-liked location for swimming and sunbathing due to its calm seas and fine white sand.

A Small island known as **Isla Contoy** is situated off the coast of Cancun. Sea turtles, dolphins, and manta rays are among the many species of marine life that call this protected nature reserve home. Visitors may go snorkeling and take an island tour to get a close-up look at the aquatic life.

**Cancun Underwater Museum**: This amazing site is located off the coast of Cancun and exhibits over 500 life-size sculptures submerged in the ocean. To see the sculptures up close and learn about the artist's conservation efforts, visitors may go scuba diving or snorkeling.

**Parasailing** is a well-liked activity in Cancun that gives guests the chance to fly above the glistening waves and take in breath-taking vistas of the shoreline. In Cancun, a number of businesses provide parasailing trips.

**Jet skiing** is another well-liked sport in Cancun, giving tourists the opportunity to jet over the glistening waves and take in the breathtaking surroundings. In Cancun, a number of businesses provide jet ski excursions and rentals.

Cancun is a well-liked location for **snorkeling** since it is home to some of the most stunning coral reefs on earth. Visitors may go snorkeling to explore the reefs and get up close views of a wide variety of aquatic life.

**Scuba diving**: Another well-liked sport in Cancun is scuba diving, which gives tourists the ability to explore the undersea world and see a wide variety of marine species. In Cancun, there are several scuba diving trips and certification programs.

Visitors may join a **Whale shark tour** from June to September to get a close-up look with these gentle giants. Visitors are taken on cruises out to sea where they may swim with whale sharks and hear about conservation initiatives.

Cancun is a well-known fishing location with a variety of fish species, including marlin, sailfish, and tuna. Visitors who want to spend a day on the sea and try their luck at capturing these amazing fish may join a **Fishing excursion.**

## 2. Ruins from the Mayans

Cancun is well known not just for its stunning beaches and water sports, but it is also the location of some of the most amazing Mayan ruins in the whole world. The following are a some of Cancun's most well-known Mayan ruins:

One of the most well-known Mayan ruins in the world and a UNESCO World Heritage site is **Chichen Itza**. It's roughly two and a half hours from Cancun and has amazing buildings like the Great Ball Court and the Temple of Kukulcan.

**Tulum**: An hour and a half's drive from Cancun lies Tulum, a walled Mayan city on the Yucatan Peninsula. The Caribbean Sea's stunning blue seas can be seen from the ruins, which makes it a well-liked destination for tourists.

**Coba**: About two hours from Cancun, in the middle of the jungle, lies the Mayan city of Coba. It has the Nohoch Mul Pyramid, the highest Mayan pyramid on the Yucatan Peninsula, which guests may climb for breathtaking views of the surrounding rainforest.

**Ek Balam**: The Yucatan Peninsula's best-preserved Mayan ruins are found at Ek Balam, a Mayan metropolis that is roughly two hours away from Cancun. Amazing monuments like the Acropolis and the Ball Court may be seen by visitors who explore the remains.

**El Rey**: In Cancun's Hotel Zone, there is a little Mayan site called El Rey. It has a number of buildings, including a ball court, a temple, and a palace, and it gives visitors the opportunity to study about the Mayan civilization's past.

The Mayan ruins are a fantastic place to visit some of the most amazing constructions in the world and learn about the history of the Mayan culture. To learn about the importance and history of each ruin, visitors may either join guided tours or go on their own exploration. Remember to pack lots of drink, sunscreen, and good walking shoes since the ruins may become rather hot.

## 3. Attractions and theme parks

Cancun is home to a number of theme parks and attractions that provide tourists with a distinctive and interesting experience in addition to the stunning beaches and Mayan ruins. The following list includes some of Cancun's top theme parks and tourist destinations:

A wildlife preserve called **Xcaret** is roughly an hour's drive from Cancun. It has Mayan ruins, unusual animals, subterranean waterways, and a butterfly pavilion. A stunning presentation with traditional Mexican music and dancing is also available for visitors to enjoy.

A natural aquarium called **Xel-Ha** is roughly an hour and a half's drive from Cancun. Visitors get the opportunity to dive, swim with dolphins, and explore the rainforest while there, which is also home to hundreds of different types of aquatic life.

**Adventure park Xplor** is around an hour away from Cancun. Visitors may go through the rainforest on amphibious vehicles, subterranean rivers, and zip lines.

*Selvatica*: About 30 minutes from Cancun is where you'll find Selvatica, an adventure park. There are zip lines, ATV rides, bungee swings, and a swimming cenote for guests to enjoy.

**Cancun Interactive Aquarium**: Located in Cancun's Hotel Zone, the Cancun Interactive Aquarium allows visitors to get up close and personal with a variety of aquatic animals, including dolphins, sea lions, and sharks.

**Cancun's Hotel Zone** is home to the Museo Maya de Cancun, a museum dedicated to the Mayan civilization. There are displays and items from the Mayan civilisation, including as ceramics, jewelry, and tools.

A fun and distinctive way to see Cancun's beauty and culture is to visit these theme parks and attractions. Depending on their interests and time limits, visitors may opt to visit one or more of these attractions. Many of the parks provide all-inclusive packages that include lodging, meals, and entertainment, making them a practical choice for tourists.

## 4. Nightlife and shopping

Cancun is popular for shopping and nightlife in addition to its stunning beaches, vibrant culture, and adventurous activities. Here are some of the top locations in Cancun for shopping and taking in the lively nightlife:

**La Isla retail Village**: In Cancun, La Isla Shopping Village is one of the most well-liked retail areas. It is a sizable outdoor mall with more than 150 shops, eateries, and entertainment options. Visitors may have a meal while admiring the lagoon or buy for designer labels, trinkets, and jewelry.

**Luxury Avenue** is another another upscale retail district in Cancun. It has shops like Cartier, Fendi, and Louis Vuitton among others.

**Plaza Caracol**: In Cancun's Hotel Zone, there is a retail center called Plaza Caracol. It has a variety of shops, eateries, and places to have fun, such a theater and a bowling alley.

One of Cancun's most well-known nightclubs is called **Coco Bongo**. It is renowned for its exhilarating performances, which include dancers, acrobats, and music from many periods and genres. A memorable night out and limitless beverages are available to visitors.

**Mandala Nightclub**: Cancun is home to another well-liked nightclub called Mandala. It has a rooftop patio with breathtaking city views as well as a number of themed suites, each with their own music and mood.

**Mercado 28**: Located in the heart of Cancun, Mercado 28 is a classic Mexican market. It's a nice spot to purchase trinkets, locally manufactured goods, and meals like tacos and tamales.

**Hacienda Tequila**: Located in Cancun's Hotel Zone, Hacienda Tequila is a tequila museum and bar. Visitors may sample several tequila varieties while learning about the spirit's manufacturing history.

Whether you're searching for high-end luxury labels or traditional Mexican crafts, a crazy night out at a nightclub, or a calm evening sipping tequila, Cancun's shopping and entertainment culture has something for everyone. Visitors have the option of booking a trip that includes transportation and a guide or exploring these locations on their own.

# V. Let's eat in Cancun

In this section, we will explore the best of Mexican Cuisine to enjoy in Cancun, popular dishes, street food and best restaurants to have them in 2023

## 1. Traditional Mexican cuisine

Traditional Mexican food is one of the greatest ways to explore Cancun's rich cultural history. Local food is a fusion of indigenous foods and Spanish influences, reflecting the many areas of Mexico. Here are a few typical Mexican cuisine you have to eat when you're in Cancun:

**Tacos al pastor**: In Mexico, tacos al pastor are a common street snack. It is made out of thinly sliced marinated pork that is roasted on a spit and served with pineapple, onion, and cilantro on little tortillas.

**Chiles en nogada** is a seasonal meal that is often served in Mexico during the country's Independence Day festivities. It is made out of roasted poblano peppers that have been filled with a variety of meat, fruits, and spices. A creamy walnut sauce and pomegranate seeds have been added on top.

**Pozole**: A hearty stew cooked with hominy, meat (often pig), and a combination of herbs and spices is known as pozole. It often comes with garnishes like avocado, radishes, and lime.

**Tamales**: In Mexico, tamales are a common dish. They are formed of corn dough that has been stuffed with a variety of ingredients, including cheese, chicken, pork, or vegetables, and then wrapped in corn husks before being steamed.

Avocado, tomato, onion, lime juice, cilantro, and mashed avocado are combined to make a dip known as **Guacamole** . It is often paired with tortilla chips or used as a garnish for tacos and other Mexican food.

**Mezcal**: Produced in various parts of Mexico, mezcal is a sort of agave-based alcoholic beverage. It is often consumed plain or in cocktails and has a distinctly smokey taste.

**Horchata**: Rice, almonds, and cinnamon are combined to make this energizing beverage. It's a preferred beverage in Mexico, particularly on hot summer days.

Traditional Mexican food is served in many Cancun restaurants, and tourists have a variety of alternatives to select from, including anything from street sellers to fine dining establishments. Taquerias—small eateries with a focus on tacos and other typical Mexican fare—are also often seen. Overall, sampling authentic Mexican food while in Cancun is a must-do experience.

## 2. Renowned eateries and bars to done in 2023

Visitors visiting Cancun have access to a broad range of eating alternatives, from high-end restaurants to regional street food vendors. You may visit the following well-known eateries and pubs during your stay:

Traditional Mexican and Yucatecan food is served at **La Habichuela**, a restaurant. Having been in business for more than 40 years, the restaurant is renowned for its mouthwatering fare, including cochinita pibil (slow-roasted pig) and chiles en nogada.

The greatest steaks in Cancun can be found at **Harry's Prime Steakhouse & Raw Bar**, a luxurious restaurant. Fresh fish meals are offered at the restaurant's raw bar as well.

**Restaurant Hacienda Sisal**: Hacienda Sisal specializes on authentic Yucatecan food. The eatery offers food like poc chuc (grilled pork marinated in tart orange juice) and sopa de lima (chicken and lime soup), and is housed in a lovely hacienda-style edifice.

**The Surfin Burrito** is a well-known fast-food establishment that offers mouthwatering burritos, tacos, and other Mexican street cuisine. The eatery is renowned for its welcoming ambiance and reasonable costs.

Italian food is served in the restaurant and bar **Palazzo**. The eatery provides food including handmade pasta and wood-fired pizzas and has a lovely outside dining area.

**Coco Bongo**: Coco Bongo is a well-liked nightclub with a fun atmosphere and great performances. Live music, acrobatic displays, and celebrity impressions are all included at the nightclub.

**La Vaquita**: The nightclub La Vaquita is renowned for its fun atmosphere and reasonable pricing. The nightclub plays music from several genres, such as reggaeton, hip-hop, and electronic dance music (EDM).

**Mandala** is a nightclub renowned for its opulent ambiance and VIP treatment. The nightclub has bars and dance floors on many levels, as well as VIP-only rooms.

**Senor Frog's** is a well-known pub and restaurant franchise that is renowned for its jovial ambiance and exotic beverages. The Cancun location has live entertainment and is close to the beach.

These are just a handful of the many eateries and nightclubs you may check out while visiting Cancun. There is food for everyone in this thriving metropolis, whether you like traditional Mexican fare or other cuisines.

# 4. Street Food

You must taste the street food if you want to sample Cancun's authentic flavors. The street food scene in Cancun is renowned for its diversity, which includes a wide range of tastes, spices, and textures. The following are a some of the most well-liked Cancun street foods:

**Elote** is a famous snack made out of roasted corn on the cob that has been covered with mayonnaise, cheese, lime juice, and chili powder. This spicy and delicious snack is ideal for a fast nibble while traveling.

**Tostadas**: Tostadas are tortillas that have been fried or torched and are then covered with a variety of foods, including beans, chicken, beef, or seafood. The remaining toppings include lettuce, tomatoes, cheese, and salsa. This meal is ideal as a snack or light lunch.

**Tortas**: Made from a soft telera bread roll and stuffed with a variety of toppings, including meat, cheese, lettuce, tomato, avocado, and mayonnaise, tacos are a traditional Mexican sandwich. This full sandwich is ideal for lunch or supper.

**Churros**: Churros are cinnamon- and sugar-dusted pastries made of fried dough. Frequently, a side of chocolate sauce is included for dipping. This delicious delicacy is ideal as a dessert or a snack.

These are just a handful of the many street cuisines available in Cancun. It's crucial to choose clean, well-kept food carts while sampling street fare. Having cash on hand is also a smart idea as many street sellers do not take credit cards. Be daring, sample some street food, and savor Cancun's delights!

# VI. Culture and Customs

Here we will have a look at the various aspects of the rich cultural heritage of Cancun

## 1. Cultural events and festivals

Cancun is a city steeped in culture and customs, and there are several cultural events and festivals held there all year long. Here are a few of the most well-known festivals and cultural events you can attend in Cancun:

**Day of the Dead**: The Day of the Dead is a holiday that is observed on November 1st and 2nd. The festival is distinguished by vibrant parades, elaborate altars, and gifts of food and flowers. It is a time when friends and family join together to commemorate and honor their deceased loved ones.

**Carnival**: Cancun has a vibrant event called Carnival every February or March. There will be street celebrations, music, dancing, and vibrant parades throughout this period. The event, which takes place over a number of days, is a celebration of joy and life.

**Independence Day**: Mexico's Independence Day is celebrated on September 16th as a national holiday with parades, fireworks, and other events. The holiday, which honors the nation's fight for independence from Spain, is significant in Mexican history and culture.

**Guelaguetza**: Cancun also participates in this event, which is held in the state of Oaxaca. The event combines music, dance, and local cuisine as a celebration of indigenous cultures and customs. For anybody interested in Mexican culture, it is a bright and energetic celebration that must be experienced.

**Mayan Civilization Festival**: The Mayan Culture Festival honors the enduring vitality of the ancient Mayan civilization in Cancun and its environs. The celebration includes displays of Mayan artwork and crafts together with traditional music, dancing, and cuisine.

You may take part in a variety of cultural events and festivals in Cancun, to name just a few. They provide a wonderful opportunity to appreciate Mexican culture and learn about the city's rich cultural past.

## 2. Customs and Manners

As a visitor to Cancun, it is crucial to comprehend and respect the locals' traditions and manners since Mexico has a rich cultural past. Here are some manners and traditions pointers to remember:

Greetings

Mexicans tend to be kind and hospitable, and greetings between friends and relatives often include a handshake or an embrace. Using titles like "Seor" or "Seora" when addressing someone you don't know well is considered respectful.

Although Mexicans normally don't care too much about being on time, it is still considered courteous to show up for appointments and meetings on time.

Cancun is a beach location, therefore casual clothing is appropriate in most settings. When visiting holy places or attending formal occasions, it's crucial to dress modestly.

eating etiquette states that you should wait for the host to invite you to a table while eating in a restaurant. Additionally, it's considerate to keep your hands on the table rather than on your lap. In restaurants, tips are generally left at 15-20% of the bill.

Respect for elders: Respecting elders is highly valued in Mexican society. It's crucial to address them with courtesy and respect.

When conversing, Mexicans often stand near to one another, so do not be shocked if someone approaches you. Nevertheless, it's still necessary to respect others' personal space and refrain from touching or approaching strangers too closely.

**Language**

Although English is widely spoken in Mexico, the official language is Spanish, thus it is always welcomed when tourists try to speak Spanish.

You may respect the local way of life and enjoy your vacation to Cancun by adhering to these manners and traditions.

# 3. Stay Safe

Although Cancun is a relatively safe place for tourists to visit, it is still vital to exercise care when traveling there. Following are some safety recommendations for your trip to Cancun:

**Keep to the safe areas**: Cancun is a big city, and just like any other city, certain parts are safer than others. To reduce your danger of being a victim of crime, stay in the well-known tourist locations like the Hotel Zone and the downtown area.

**Use respectable transportation**: It's important to use reliable transportation providers while moving throughout Cancun. Use only authorized taxis, and if at all feasible, make transportation arrangements via your hotel or a trustworthy tour operator. It's best to avoid hailing cabs on the street, particularly after dark.

**Be mindful of your surroundings**: While exploring Cancun on foot, always be mindful of your surroundings. Avoid dimly lit locations and keep an eye out for any shady behaviour.

Whenever you feel uneasy, follow your gut and leave for a safer area.

A prevalent issue in Cancun is theft, so it's essential to take precautions to safeguard your possessions. Cash, passports, and credit cards should be kept in a hotel safe or another secure place. Keep your wallet and baggage close to your body while you're out and about, and try to avoid flashing important goods like jewelry or gadgets.

**Avoid drugs**: Possession and usage of illicit substances are both punishable by harsh fines in Mexico. Avoid purchasing or using drugs since doing so might get you into a lot of legal problems.

**Remain hydrated**: Cancun is a hot and muggy place, therefore it's crucial to do so.

Avoid excessive alcohol drinking since it may cause dehydration and affect your judgment. Instead, drink lots of water.

**Respect the laws**: To prevent difficulties in Cancun, it's crucial to abide by the city's severe laws and regulations. For instance, it is forbidden to consume alcohol on public beaches and to engage in public nudity.

Although English is widely spoken among Cancun residents, it is always welcomed when tourists make an attempt to speak Spanish. Additionally, knowing a few basic words will be useful if you ever need aid or have an emergency.

**Have a list of emergency contacts**: In case of an emergency, it's always a good idea to have a list of contacts that includes your hotel's location and phone number as well as the details for your embassy or consulate.

You are guaranteed a risk-free and pleasurable vacation to Cancun by adhering to these safety recommendations. Use cautious, be vigilant, and take safeguards to safeguard your safety and your possessions.

# VII. Practical Information for Cancun City

## 1. Climate and weather

Cancun, situated on Mexico's Yucatan Peninsula, has year-round hot and humid weather because to its tropical climate. The rainy season and the dry season are two separate seasons in Cancun. The dry season lasts from November to April, while the rainy season is from May to October.

The humidity and temperatures are at their maximum during the rainy season, and there are many showers and thunderstorms, particularly in the afternoons. If you're going at this period, you must pack an umbrella or raincoat since the rain might be intense and brief. From 75°F (24°C) to 95°F (35°C), the temperature may vary, with July and August being the warmest and muggiest months.

The best time to visit Cancun is during the dry season, which runs from November to April. This is because the weather is cooler and less humid. The ideal period for outdoor activities is between 70°F (21°C) and 85°F (29°C), when the temperature might vary. As it is also the busiest travel period, anticipate increased costs for lodging and entertainment.

Throughout the year, it's important to remain hydrated, but it's more important in the hot, muggy months. Drink lots of water and limit your consumption of alcohol and caffeine. Apply sunscreen often and dress in light, breathable materials to shield your skin from the harsh sun.

From June through November, Cancun is also subject to the hurricane season, which peaks in September and October. Although hurricanes are not common in Cancun, it is nevertheless important to pay attention to weather forecasts and heed any instructions or cautions given by local authorities.

In conclusion, Cancun has two distinct seasons: a rainy season from May to October, and a dry season from November to April. During hurricane season, it's crucial to maintain hydration, dress comfortably, periodically apply sunscreen, and keep an eye on the weather forecasts.

## 2. How to navigate Cancun

Depending on your travel requirements and budget, Cancun offers a variety of transportation choices to assist you navigate about the city.

**Taxis**: In Cancun, taxis are by far the most practical and accessible form of transportation. Taxis are simple to find on the streets, and your hotel can even set one up for you. Although Cancun's taxis are usually secure and metered, it is wise to double check the fare with the driver before setting off on your trip. Keep little bills on hand since drivers sometimes lack the necessary change for larger sums.

**Buses and colectivos (minivans)**, which travel around the city and the neighboring regions, make up Cancun's public transportation system. The colectivos are somewhat more costly than the buses, which have prices that range from 10 to 12 pesos. These operate more often and provide more route flexibility while not having air conditioning. It is essential to remember that, particularly during peak hours, the public transit system may be congested and unpleasant.

**Car rental**: If you want to go beyond of Cancun's city boundaries, this is a great alternative. The Cancun International Airport has a number of automobile rental businesses, and most hotels also provide rental options. Cancun has well-kept roadways, and it is connected to other well-known locations via a number of toll routes. It is crucial to remember that Cancun's traffic may be congested, particularly around rush hour.

**Renting bicycles** is a fun and environmentally responsible way to see Cancun's beaches and attractions. There are several rental businesses that provide bicycles at reasonable prices, and the city has designated bike lanes everywhere. It is crucial to observe traffic laws and pay attention to other drivers on the road.

**Walking**: Cancun is a pedestrian-friendly city, so exploring the nearby markets, stores, and restaurants on foot is a great idea. There are several walkways and pedestrian crossings throughout the Hotel Zone, which is a large stretch of road. However, walking may be difficult in the hot and muggy months, so it's important to drink enough of water and wear supportive footwear.

Taxis, public transit, car and bicycle rentals, walking, and public transportation are all available in Cancun. Public transit is the most cost-effective option, but taxis are the most practical and readily accessible. Bicycles are an eco-friendly and enjoyable way to explore the city, while renting a vehicle is a great choice for traveling beyond the city boundaries. Exploring the neighborhood's attractions on foot is another excellent choice.

## 3. Currency and Money Exchange rate

Understanding the local currency and available methods of conversion is crucial when making travel plans to Cancun. Here are some useful details about money and currency exchange in Cancun:

## Currency

The Mexican peso (MXN) is the country of Mexico's official currency. For minor purchases like souvenirs, cabs, and street food, it is advised to have some pesos on hand. However, the majority of popular tourist destinations in Cancun also take US dollars, especially for more expensive items like hotel bills, excursions, and activities. It's vital to remember that purchasing using US dollars may not give as good an exchange rate as paying with pesos.

## Money Exchange

Cancun offers a variety of possibilities for money exchange. When arriving at the airport, one alternative is to convert currencies at one of the many accessible kiosks. The exchange rates at the airport, however, may not be as good as those found in other parts of the city, therefore it is advised to only exchange a limited quantity of cash there.

The usage of ATMs, which are extensively dispersed around Cancun, provides an additional option. To make sure your ATM card will function in Mexico and to learn about potential costs for foreign withdrawals, it is crucial to contact your bank in advance.

In Cancun, you may find money exchange kiosks at the majority of the main tourist attractions and commercial malls. Comparing exchange rates across various booths is advised, and you should be informed of any commission or service costs that can be assessed.

## Cards — Credit

at Cancun, credit cards are commonly accepted, notably at popular tourist locations, hotels, and dining establishments. To prevent any problems with card use, it is advised to bring cash with you for minor transactions and to let your bank know in advance of your trip.

A combination of Mexican pesos and US dollars should be carried for various sorts of transactions, and it is crucial to be aware of exchange rates and taxes while changing money in Cancun.

# 4. Safety and health

To guarantee a secure and pleasurable vacation, it's important to take certain health and safety measures while visiting Cancun. Here are some helpful tidbits concerning Cancun's health and safety:

## Health

It is advised to speak with a healthcare professional to make sure you have all the required immunizations before going to Cancun. Furthermore, it's critical to take preventative measures to avoid mosquito bites, such as wearing long sleeves and trousers and using insect repellent with DEET.

Additionally, as Cancun's tap water is not thought to be safe for ingestion, it is advised to only consume bottled water or water that has been adequately cleansed. Avoiding beverages containing ice cubes that could have been prepared with tap water is also a part of this.

There are a number of hospitals and clinics in Cancun, some of which have English-speaking personnel, for any medical situations. It is advised to obtain travel health insurance and to be aware of any potential uncovered medical expenses.

**Safety**

Although Cancun is usually thought of as a safe vacation destination, it is crucial to exercise cautious. It is advised to avoid carrying a lot of cash or valuables while out and about and to stick to well-lit, busy places. It is also advised to utilize only authorized taxis and to be alert of possible frauds like phony tour operators or taxi scams.

When swimming in the water, it's crucial to exercise caution since there might be powerful currents and rip tides. Always stay in the approved swimming areas and heed any safety advice or cautions given by lifeguards.

Emergency services in Cancun may be reached via 911.

A safe and happy vacation to Cancun may be guaranteed by taking the required health and safety measures.

# VIII. Day Trips and Excursions

## 1. Nearby islands and beaches

Why not take a day excursion to one of the surrounding islands or beaches if you want to get away from the hectic metropolis of Cancun? A day trip and excursion itinerary to some of the top local islands and beaches is provided below:

### Isle Mujeres

Isla Mujeres, which is just a short boat trip from Cancun, is a must-see location. Take the boat to Isla Mujeres from Gran Puerto Cancun or Puerto Juarez to start your day. Rent a golf cart or a bike when you get there and explore the island's lovely beaches, such Playa Norte, which is renowned for its pristine seas and breathtaking sunsets. Additionally, you may go to the Garrafon Natural Reef Park, where you can zipline, go snorkeling, and relax in the infinity pool with stunning views of the Caribbean Sea.

## Cozumel

Another neighboring island that is worthwhile seeing is Cozumel. A boat from Playa del Carmen or a 45-minute flight from Cancun are also options. Rent a vehicle or scooter when you get there to explore the island's stunning beaches and attractions, such Chankanaab National Park, where you can snorkel and scuba dive to see the coral reefs and marine life. You may discover more about the history and culture of the island by going visiting the Cozumel Museum.

## Tulum

Tulum is an excellent choice for a day trip if you have an interest in history and culture. The Tulum Archaeological Site, which has well-preserved Mayan ruins overlooking the Caribbean Sea, is situated approximately 80 miles south of Cancun. After seeing the ruins, go to the neighboring beach to unwind and go swimming in the clear waters. A natural swimming hole where you may dive and explore underwater caverns is close by called the Gran Cenote.

## Playa del Carmen

A lively beach town called Playa del Carmen is roughly an hour's drive south of Cancun. To get there, you may take a bus or hire a vehicle. When you get there, take a walk down Fifth Avenue, which is the town's major pedestrian strip and is surrounded by stores, eateries, and bars. Additionally, you may go to the Xcaret Park, where you can explore Mexican culture and history while snorkeling in coral reefs and swimming in subterranean rivers.

## Puerto Morelos

Puerto Morelos, a lovely fishing community approximately 20 miles south of Cancun, has a more laid-back and relaxing ambiance than Cancun's vibrant nightlife. You may unwind on the beach, go diving or snorkeling at the adjacent coral reef, or head to the neighboring Crococun Zoo to observe crocodiles, monkeys, and other animals.

Prepare yourself for a day of adventure and leisure on some of the most stunning islands and beaches in the Caribbean by remembering to take sunscreen, comfy shoes, and your camera!

## 2. Parks and Ecological Reserves

A day excursion to one of the neighboring ecological reserves or parks is essential if you're hoping to see Cancun and the surrounding area's natural splendor. A recommended day trip itinerary visiting some of the best parks and natural reserves in the region is provided below:

Visit the Sian Ka'an Biosphere Reserve early in the day; it's roughly two hours south of Cancun. Beautiful beaches, lagoons, and wetlands are found in this protected region, which is also home to a wide variety of species, including jaguars, monkeys, and sea turtles. Explore on your own or join a tour to learn more about the area's distinctive environment and animals.

After that, go to the Riviera Maya's neighboring Xel-Ha Park, a natural aquarium. Here, you may relax on the beach, go swimming and snorkeling, and explore the park's natural pools and lagoons. Other activities available at the site include ziplining, cliff leaping, and kayaking.

Visit the Aktun Chen Natural Park after lunch; it's roughly 30 minutes from Xel-Ha. This park is well-known for both its impressive limestone structures and its enormous subterranean river network. Visit the tunnels and caverns on a guided tour, or just stroll through the thick vegetation of the park and admire the scenery.

The Crococun Zoo, which is around 45 minutes from Aktun Chen, is a great place to conclude your day. Numerous crocodiles, snakes, and other reptiles live at this unusual zoo, along with monkeys, deer, and other animals. Explore the park on your own or join a guided tour to learn more about the creatures and their surroundings.

There are other additional natural reserves and parks in the region to visit, and this schedule may be altered based on your interests and the time you have available. For trekking and outdoor activities, remember to pack lots of water, sunscreen, bug repellant, as well as appropriate clothes and footwear.

## 3. Historic Places and Landmarks

When visiting Cancun, you really must see some of the adjacent historic towns and attractions if you have any interest in history, architecture, or culture. To make the most of your time, use the following itinerary for a day trip and an excursion:

**Chichen Itza**: This historic city is roughly 120 miles west of Cancun and is a UNESCO World Heritage site. Some of the most stunning Mayan remains in Mexico may be seen there, including the famous Kukulcan Pyramid, also known as El Castillo. You may learn about the ruins' importance and history by taking a guided tour.

**Tulum**: This picturesque coastal town is located around 80 miles south of Cancun and is well-known for its well-preserved Mayan ruins that gaze out over the Caribbean Sea. You should visit the Tulum ruins, and you should also spend some time taking in the town's lovely beaches and lively culture.

**Coba**: A second extinct Mayan city, Coba lies roughly 100 miles west of Cancun and has a remarkable system of raised stone pathways connecting its numerous constructions. Nohoch Mul, the highest building in Coba, is almost 140 feet tall and provides breathtaking views of the forest surroundings.

Approximately 100 miles west of Cancun lies the quaint colonial town of **Valladolid**, which is renowned for its attractive streets, stunning buildings, and extensive history. You may tour the town's stunning cathedrals and plazas, go to the San Bernardino de Siena Convent, and eat some of the regional food.

**Ek Balam**: The spectacular acropolis of this historic Mayan city, which is roughly 100 miles west of Cancun, is noteworthy for its detailed carvings and sculptures. The main building's summit may be reached for expansive views of the surrounding landscape.

It is preferable to reserve a guided tour that will take you to many locations and provide you detailed comments along the way if you want to make the most of your day trip.

# Conclusion

## Final thoughts on Cancun

In conclusion, Cancun is a place that really offers everything. There is something for everyone, from its breathtaking beaches and beautiful blue oceans to its rich history and culture. The city is a great location for tourists of all budgets because to its accessibility and diversity of lodging options, which range from affordable hostels to opulent resorts.

Cancun has a wide variety of attractions, including water sports, amusement parks, and historical sites. Additionally, traditional Mexican meals and delectable street food should not be missed by foodies.

Even though there are certain safety issues to be aware of, taking reasonable safety measures may guarantee a safe and pleasurable journey. The city's pleasant weather and temperate environment are other factors that make it popular year-round.

Overall, Cancun is a place that every visitor should put on their bucket list. It really is a paradise worth visiting with its stunning natural surroundings, rich history and culture, and limitless chances for adventure and leisure.

## Alternative sources and suggestions

**Cancun International Airport**: Information about flights, transportation, and airport services may be found on the airport's official website.

**Mexican Tourism Board**: The Mexican Tourism Board offers helpful information, such as travel warnings, safety advice, and cultural activities, for tourists planning trips to Cancun.

**The Cancun City Tour** is a terrific way to visit all of the city's top sights in a single day while still having the freedom to go at your own leisure.

**Mexican Caribbean Travel Association**: The Mexican Caribbean Travel Association offers information on other neighboring locations that may be visited as day excursions from Cancun, such as Playa del Carmen and Isla Mujeres.

Travelers may organize a memorable and delightful vacation to Cancun by utilizing these tools and suggestions, making the most of all the city has to offer.

## HAVE A MEMORABLE TRIP

Printed in Great Britain
by Amazon

25035842R00066